AF433542

That Elf Ain't On the Shelf Coloring Story Book

Year after year
around
Christmas time
a little guy
dressed in green
that we call
an elf
gets placed
on a shelf
Does he remain
there?
This would be
ever so
rare!

This curious elf
on the shelf
did not stay
he is hiding
behind an
ornament
and
he is
ready
to
PLAY !

So
into a super sweet
ice cream cone
this naughty
elf did go.
He does not
belong
in my treat.
I can only see
his arms
and his
feet!

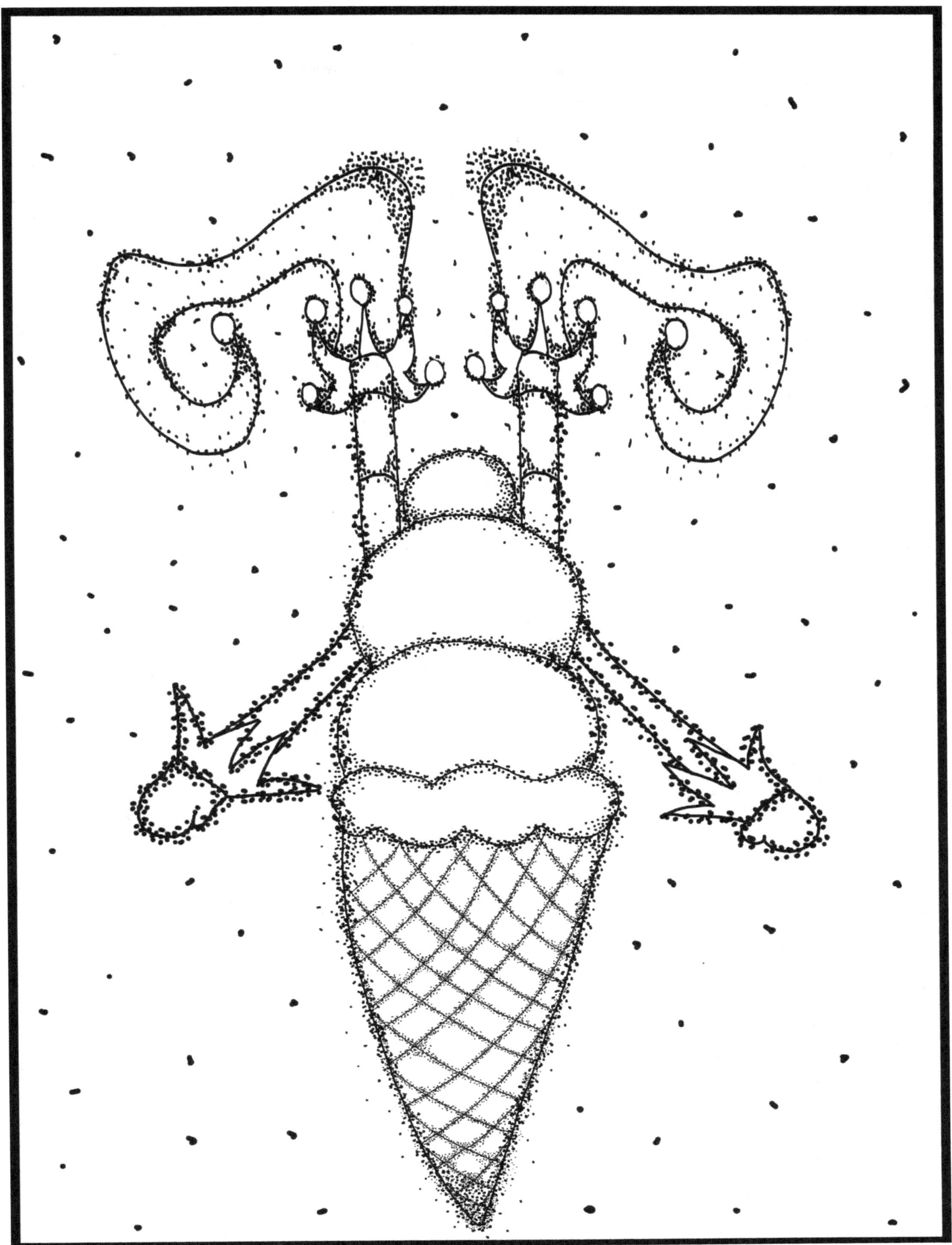

Into
a jar
this
elf
would now go
and
his
next
move would
not take him
too far.

Look,
Oh Look
the
Elf
is outside.
Will
he come
back in?
He must
decide !

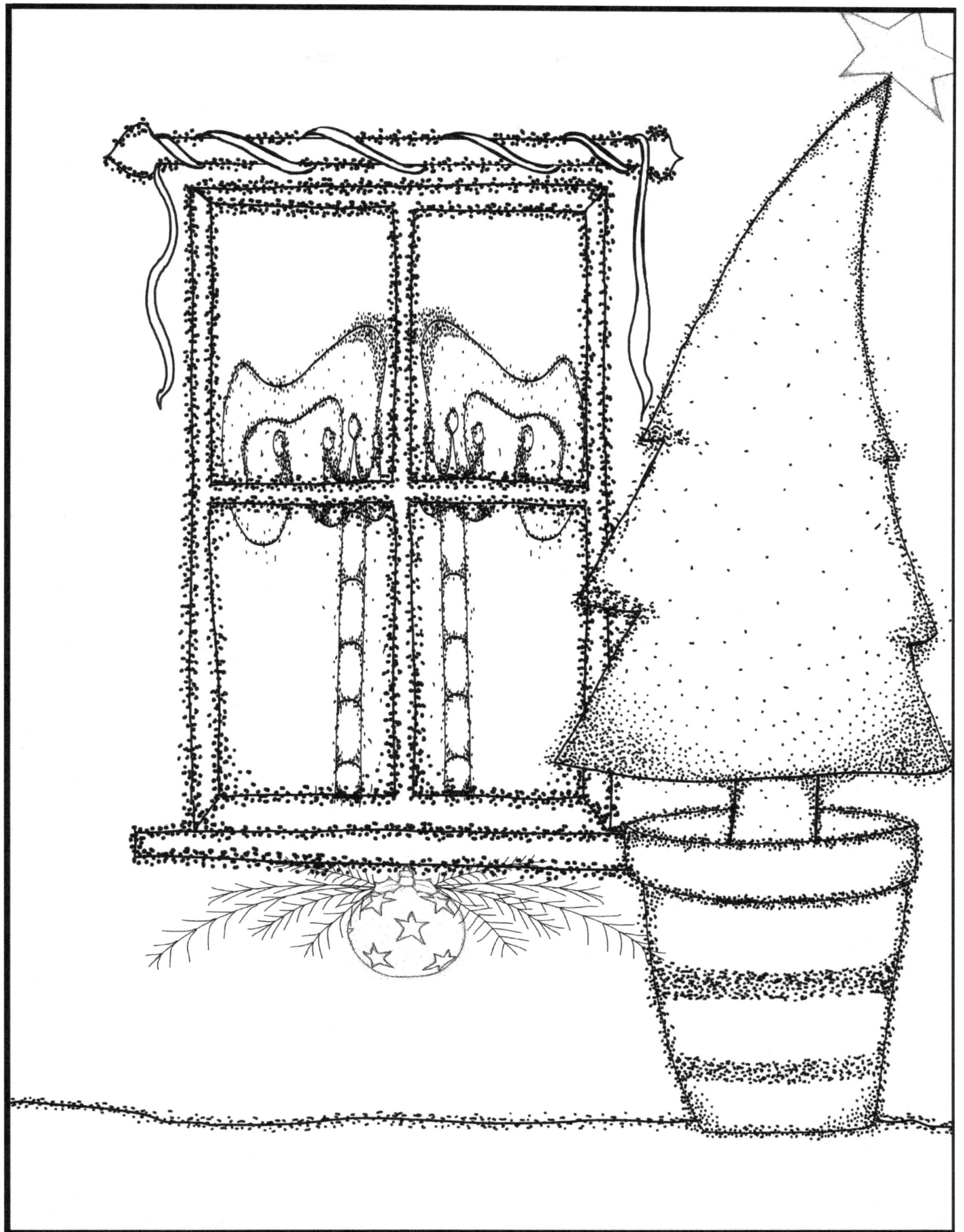

He stayed
out there
all night,
remaining
in sight.
Where would
he be at
Dawn's
first
light?

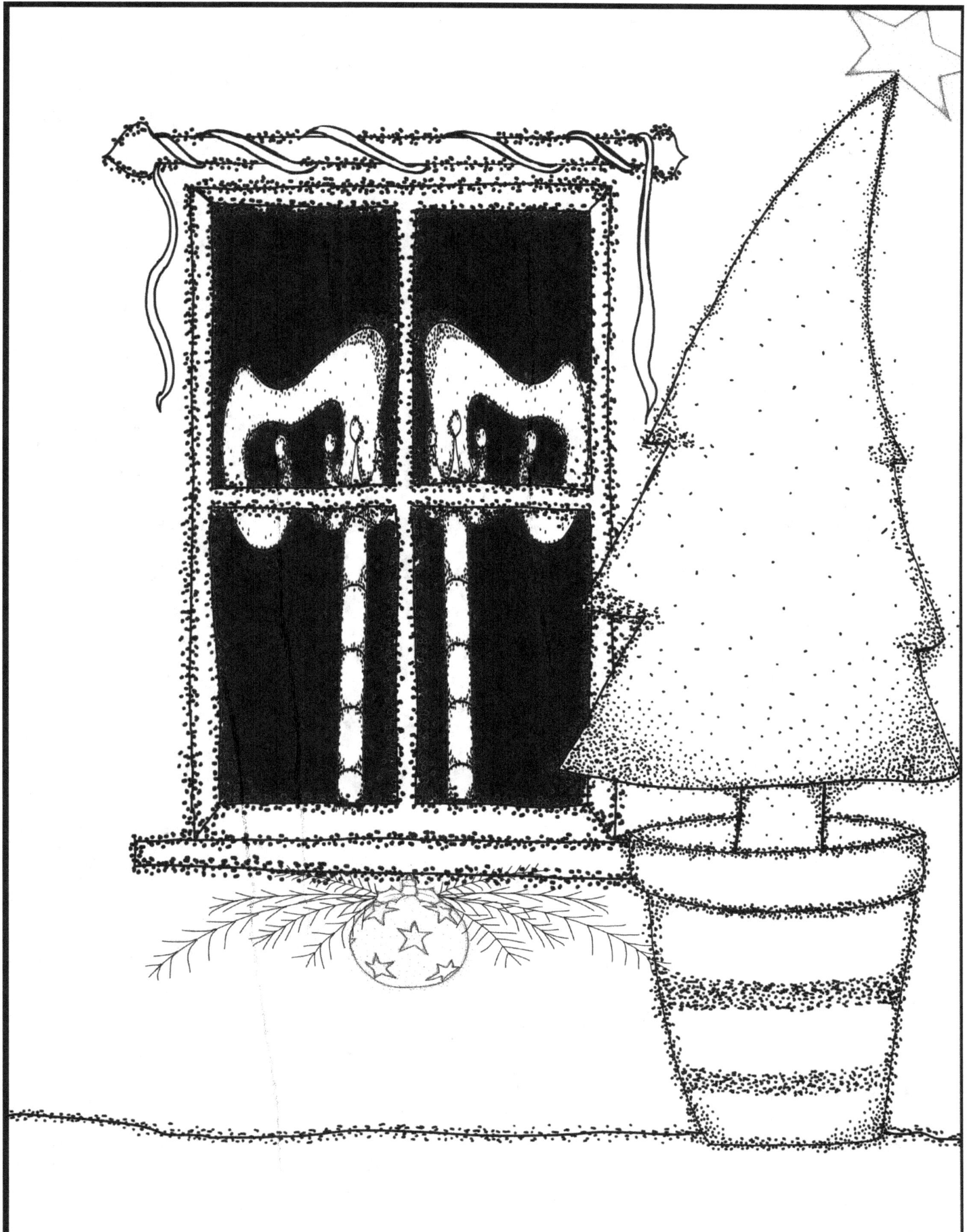

Oh elf
in
and
on
the
sun
you
should
not
be !

Open wide
and say,
"ELF"
No,No,No
Oh Elf
get
back
on
your
shelf !

This naughty
Elf laughs,
"Oh Tee,
Hee, Hee,
Hee"
and off he
goes to the
dog food
bowl for some...

Dog Food Diving

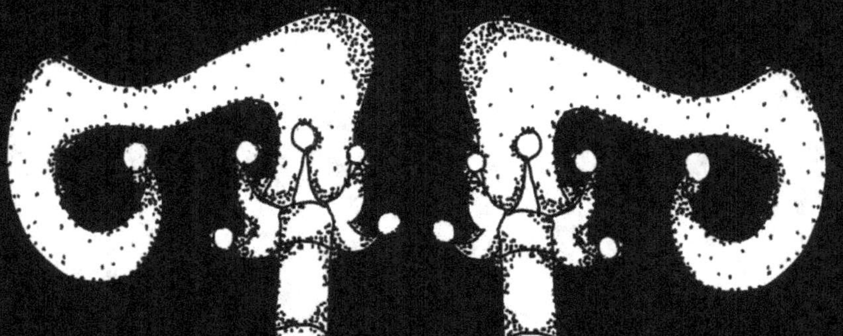

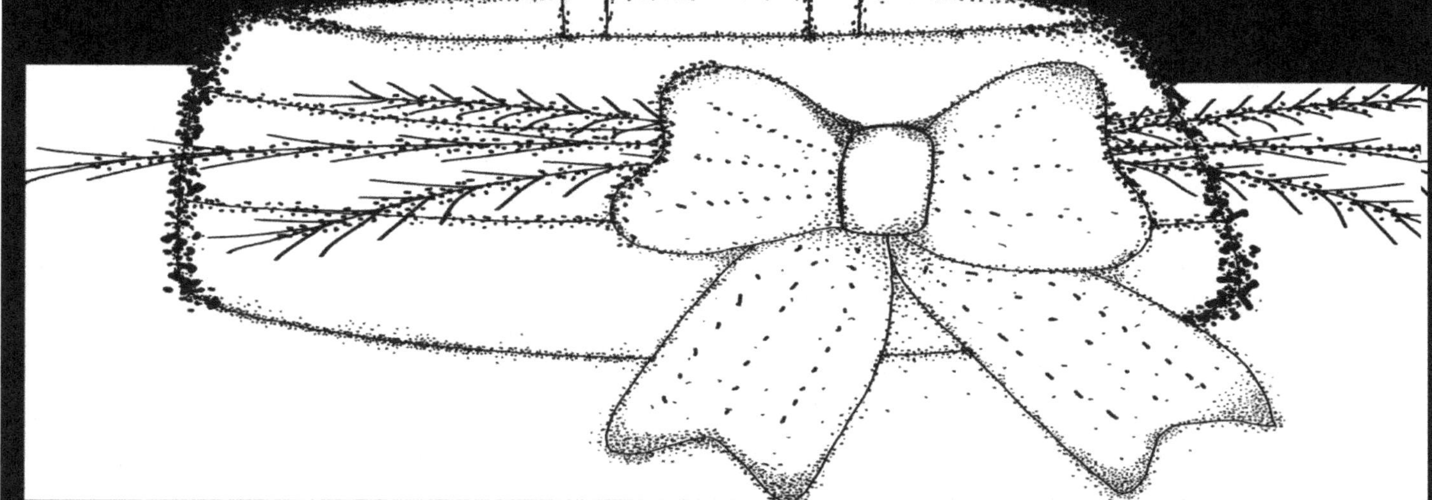

Oh
this
Elf
just
can't
stay
out
of the
sweets

Double
the
Pleasure
Double
the
Fun
With two
Naughty
Elves
and not
just
one !

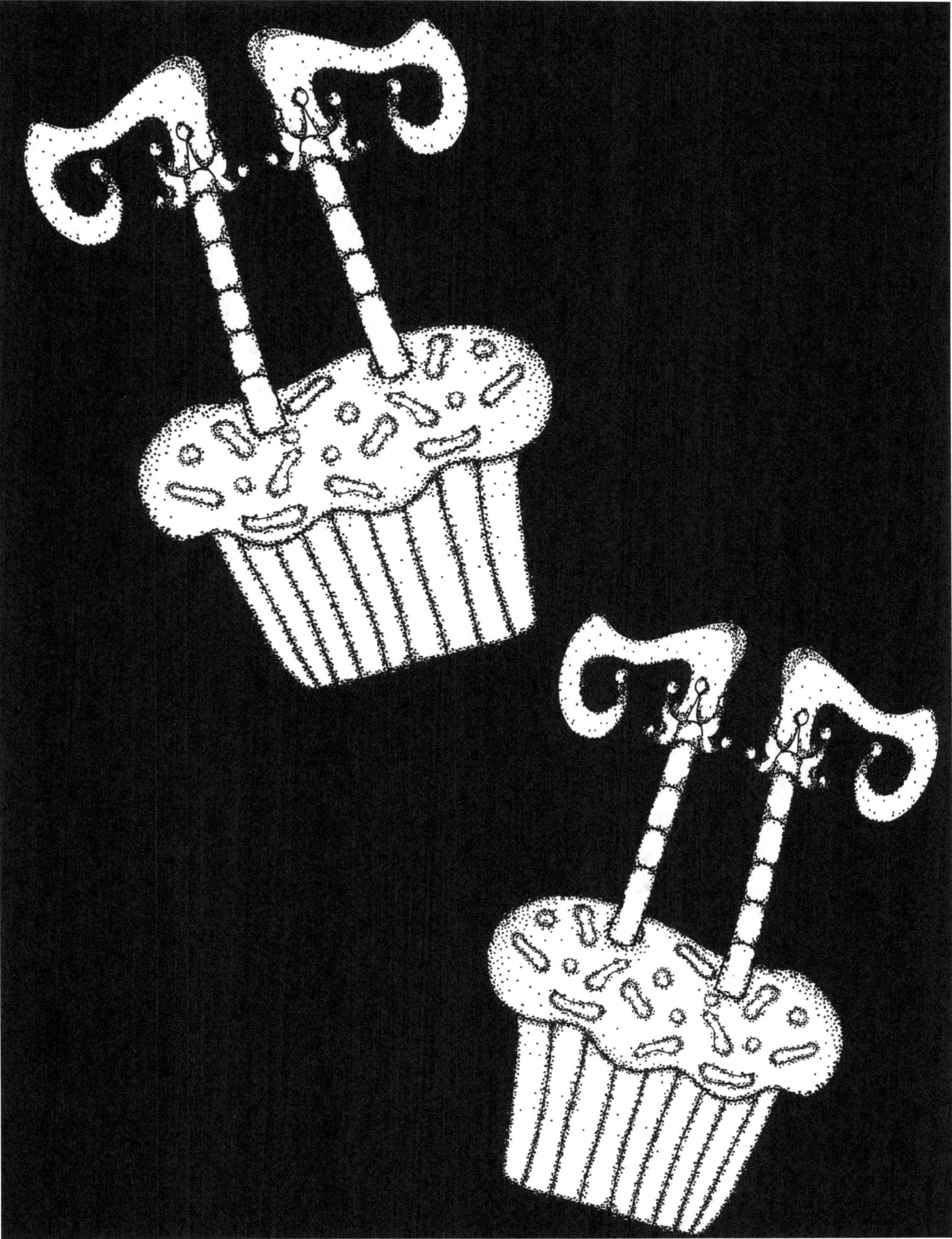

Sweet Tweet
has spent too
much time
with that
Elf
and
is
turning into
an
Elf
himself !

Oh the man
in the moon
has a
frown on his
face.
That ELF
should
go home
and not
cause trouble
in outer
space!

Into
your
cup
that
darn
Elf
will go.
Oh no,
no, no
and
NO!

He dove
down
deep
into cups
one
two,
and
three !

Oh
little
ELF
You
Do
NOT
Scare
Me !

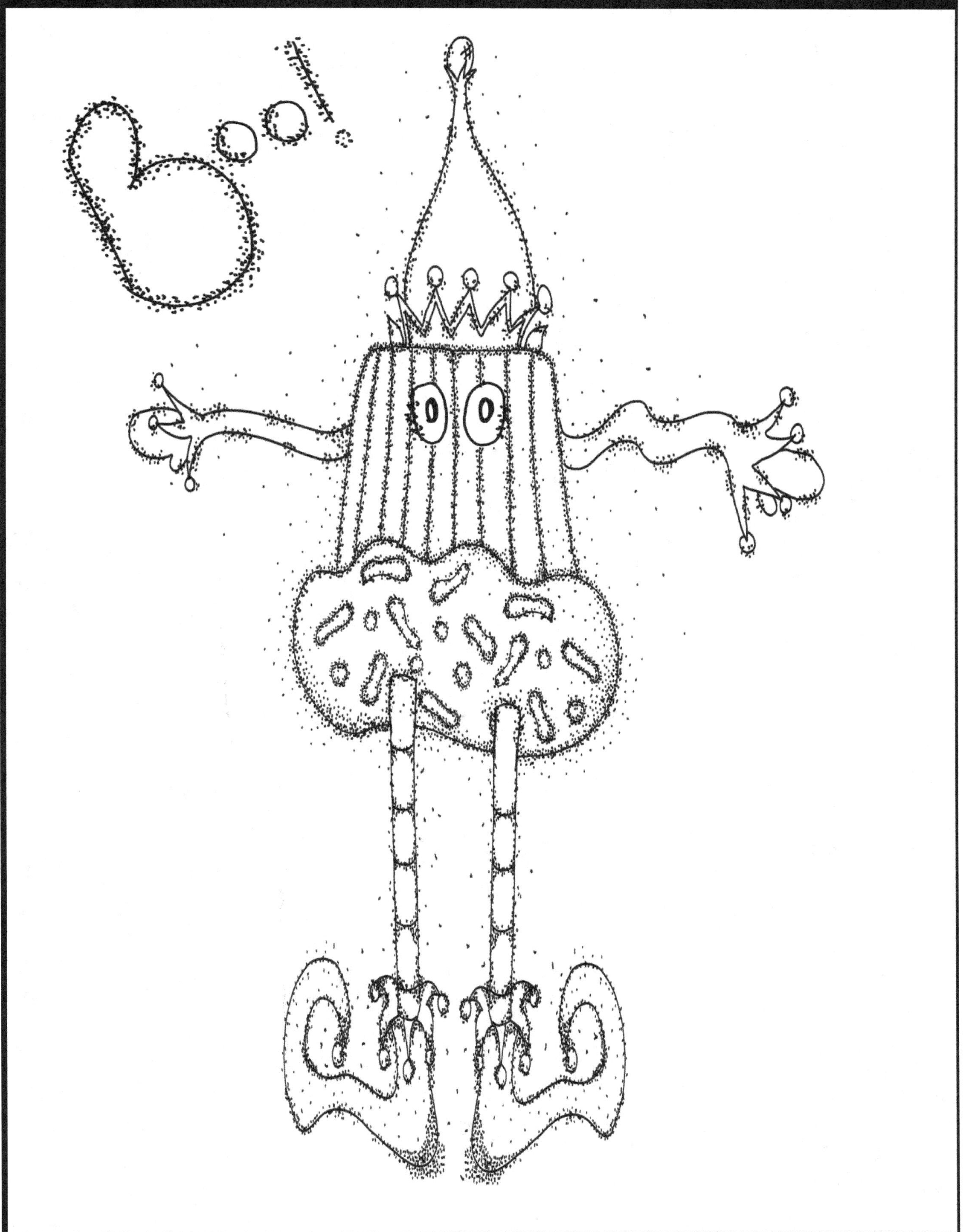
Boo!

I
was
sunnyside
up
until
that Elf
took a
jump
off
the shelf !

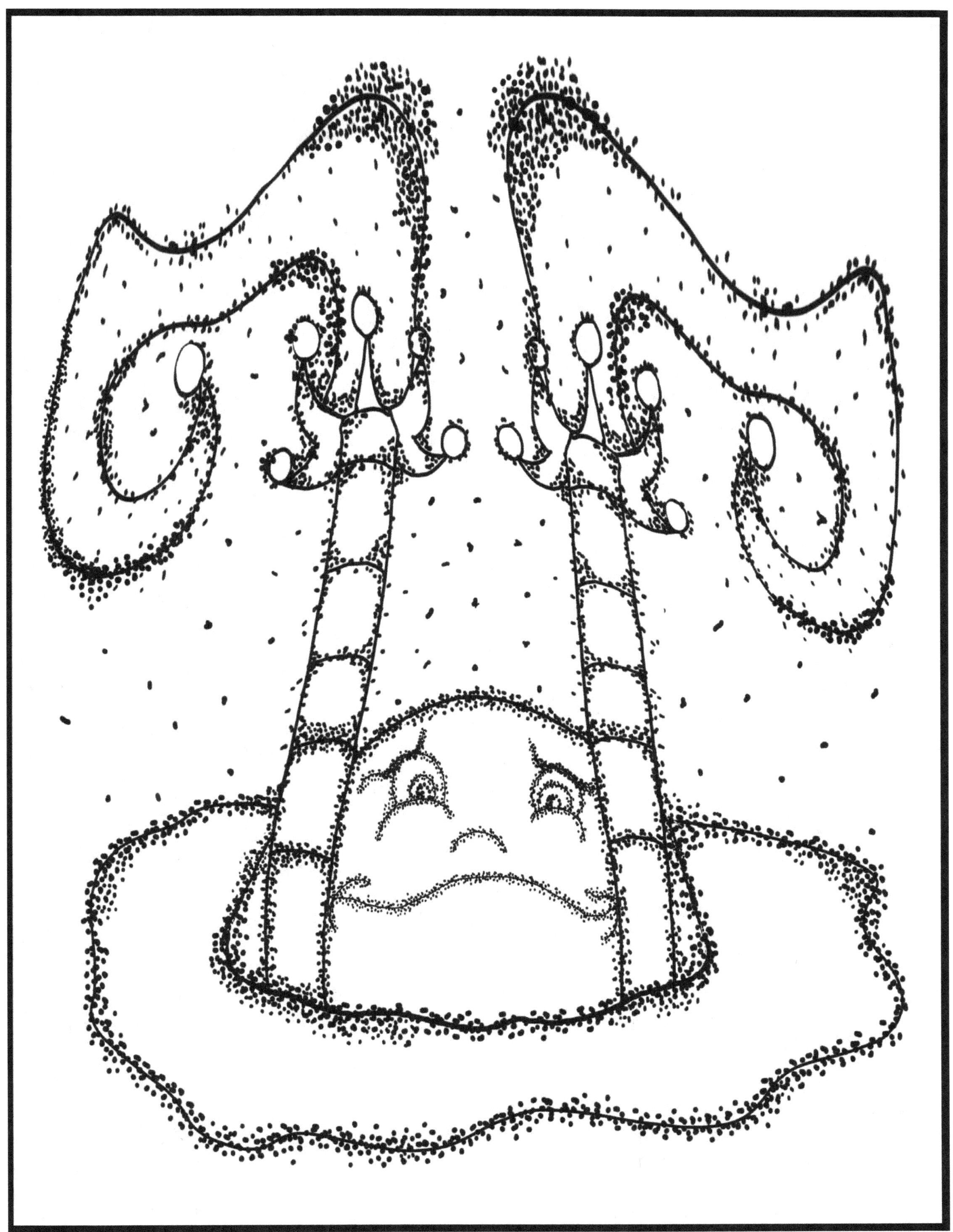

This Elf
Loves
Eggs
and
that's no
joke,
but this
egg wants
him
out of
her
YOKE !

This
ELF
just
does not
care
and
could
stay
until
he
needs
air !

While
in my
bed
that
Elf
took
every sweet
dream
from my
head!

Oh, no,no,no
this is NOT
what we do
leave
the
fish alone
and
get
out,
go do
something
new!

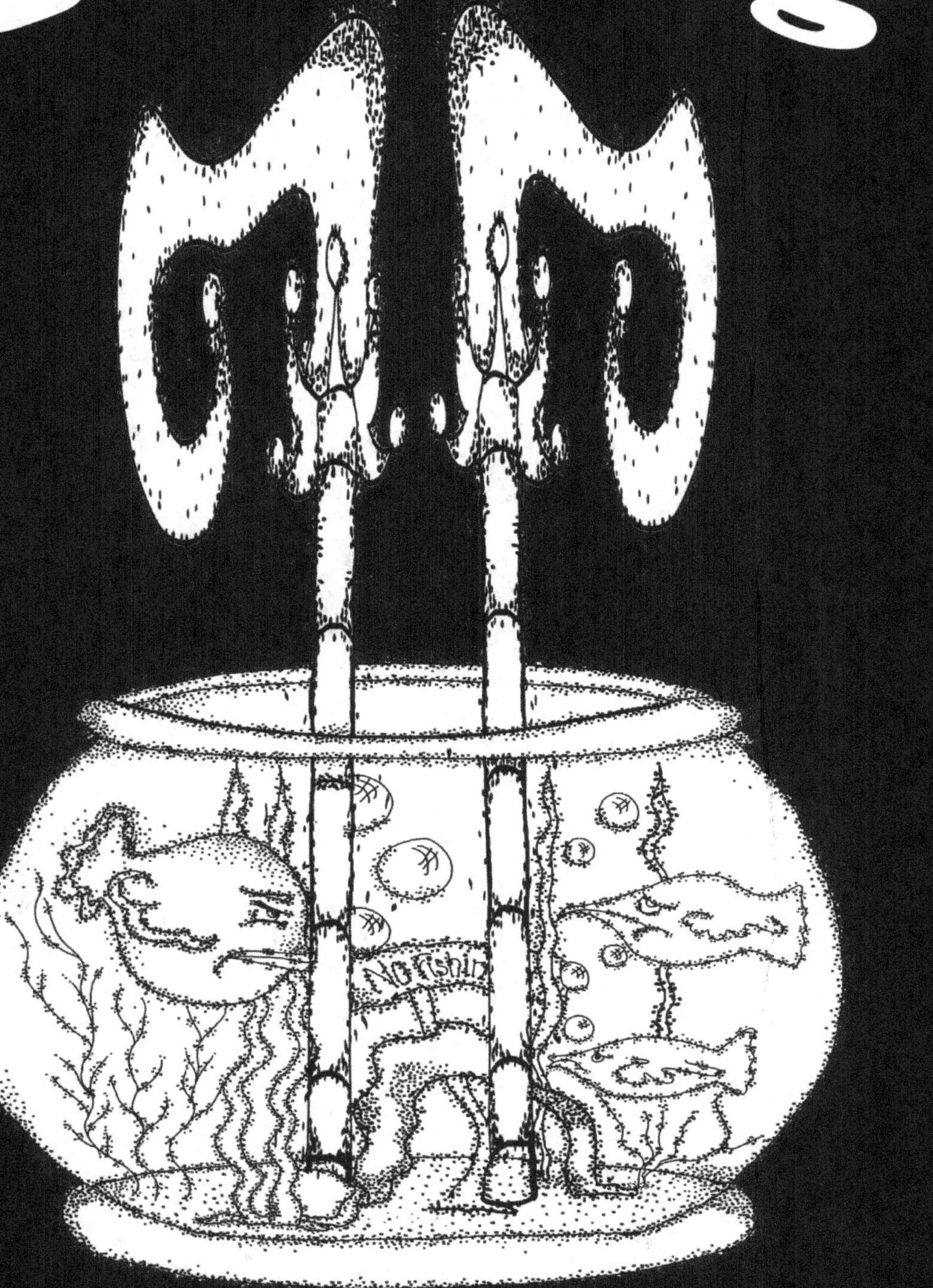
Gone Fishing
No Fishing

So into the
cookie jar
this crazy Elf goes.
Please
leave the cookies
alone!
They are NOT
for you,
they are
all
for
ME!

Christmas
cookies

OH
NO
ELF
NOT
INTO
OUR
TREE
!!!

This
ELF
simply
MUST
check
everything
OUT

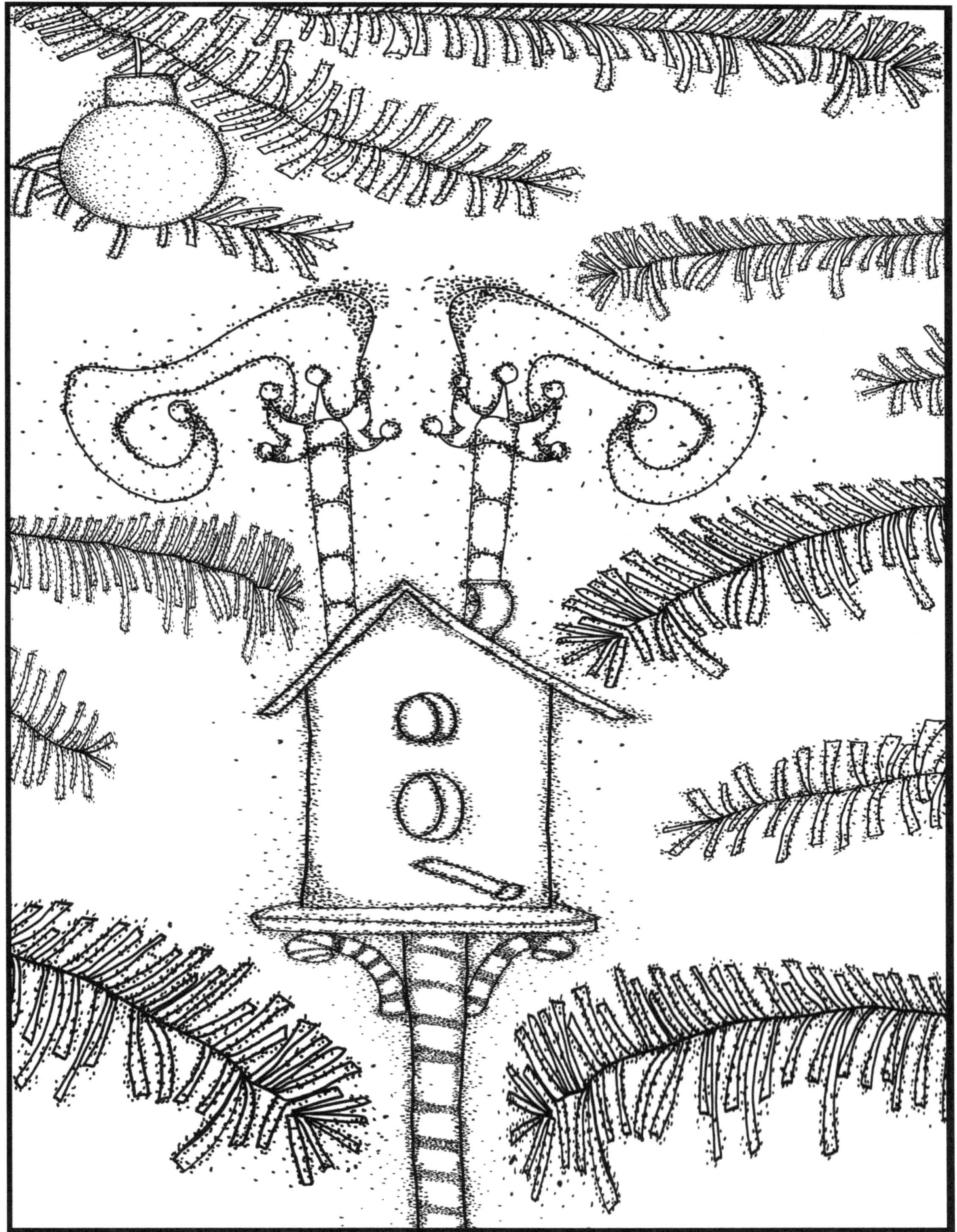

Inside
Sweet Tweet's
birdhouse
this
Elf
spends
the
night.

Oh ELf,
it is on
a shelf
you belong
get out
of Tweet's
house,
you've been
there too
long!

He
liked
it
in
there
and
would
stay
and
stay

Until
this ELF
into
our tree
got inside
so he
could just
run
away!

Oh no
no, no
Oh no

No, No,
NO
ELF
DO NOT
STEAL
OUR
TREE!
On the shelf
is where you
must be!

Oh No
No No
Oh No

He did NOT
go back on
the shelf,
not THIS
naughty ELF,
I found him
hiding
way
under
my
bed
!

He stayed
there
all day
and
all night too
just maybe
he is running
out of
strange
things
to do!

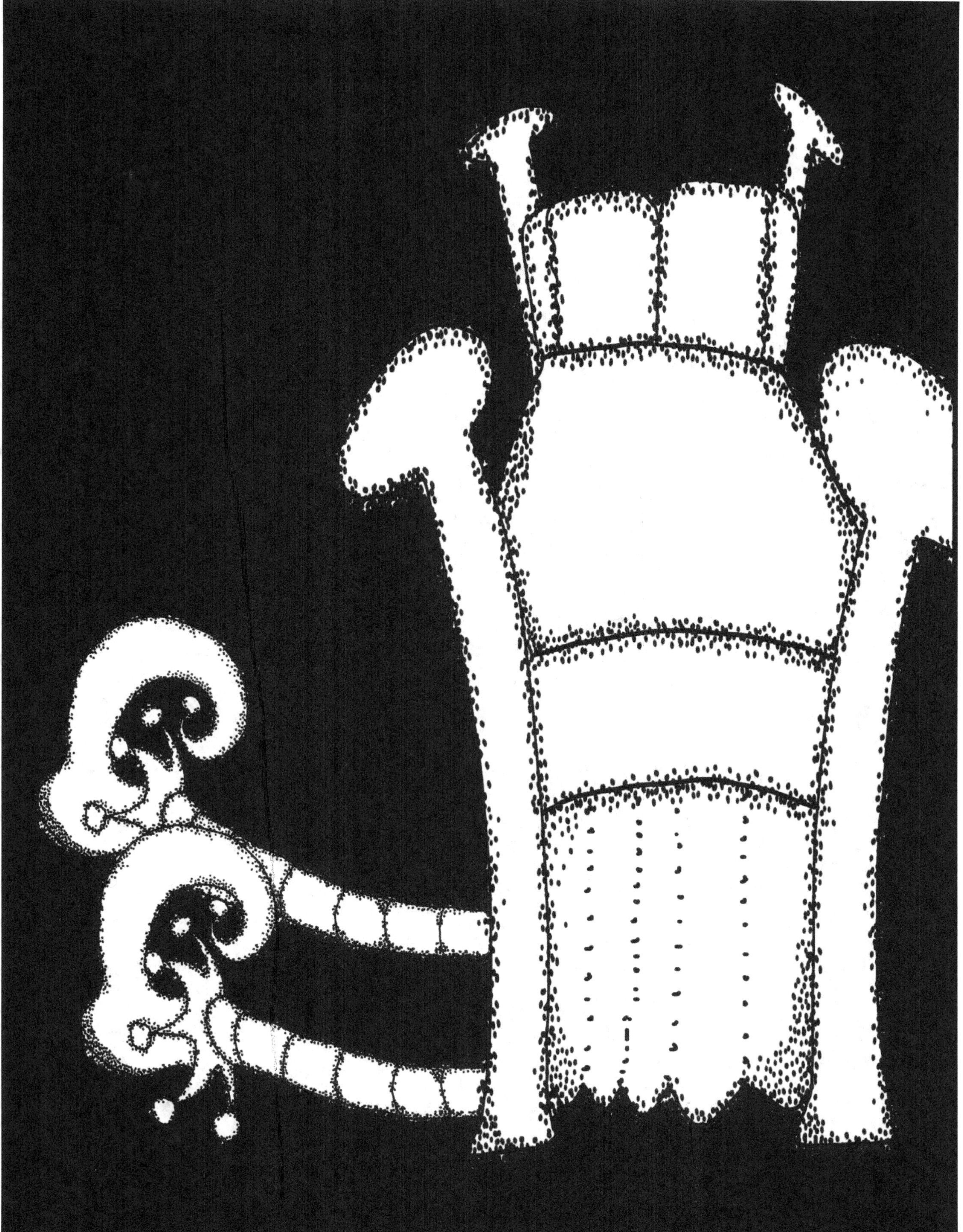

Oh no
he isn't done
yet
He's a little
bit
worried
as
he should
be........

Oh, no.......

Not a cookie!

and for
awhile
that Elf
became a
part of a
cookie
and that
cookie
would never
be the same!

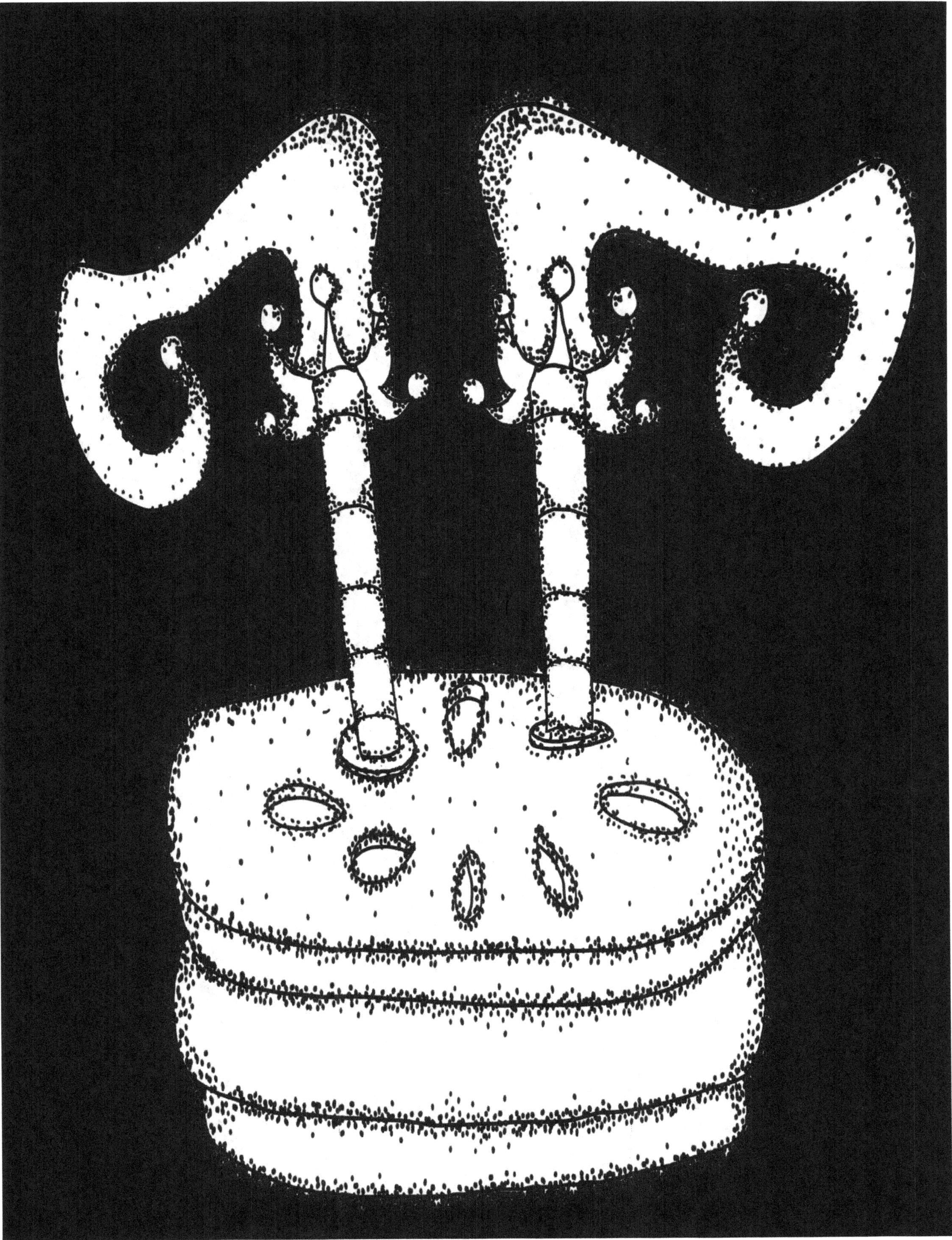

Sometimes
he isn't so
very bad
and can be
a good ELF
not making
us mad.
But never forget
you might just find
him taking a dive!

Into
the

toilet
why?
why?
OH
WHY
???

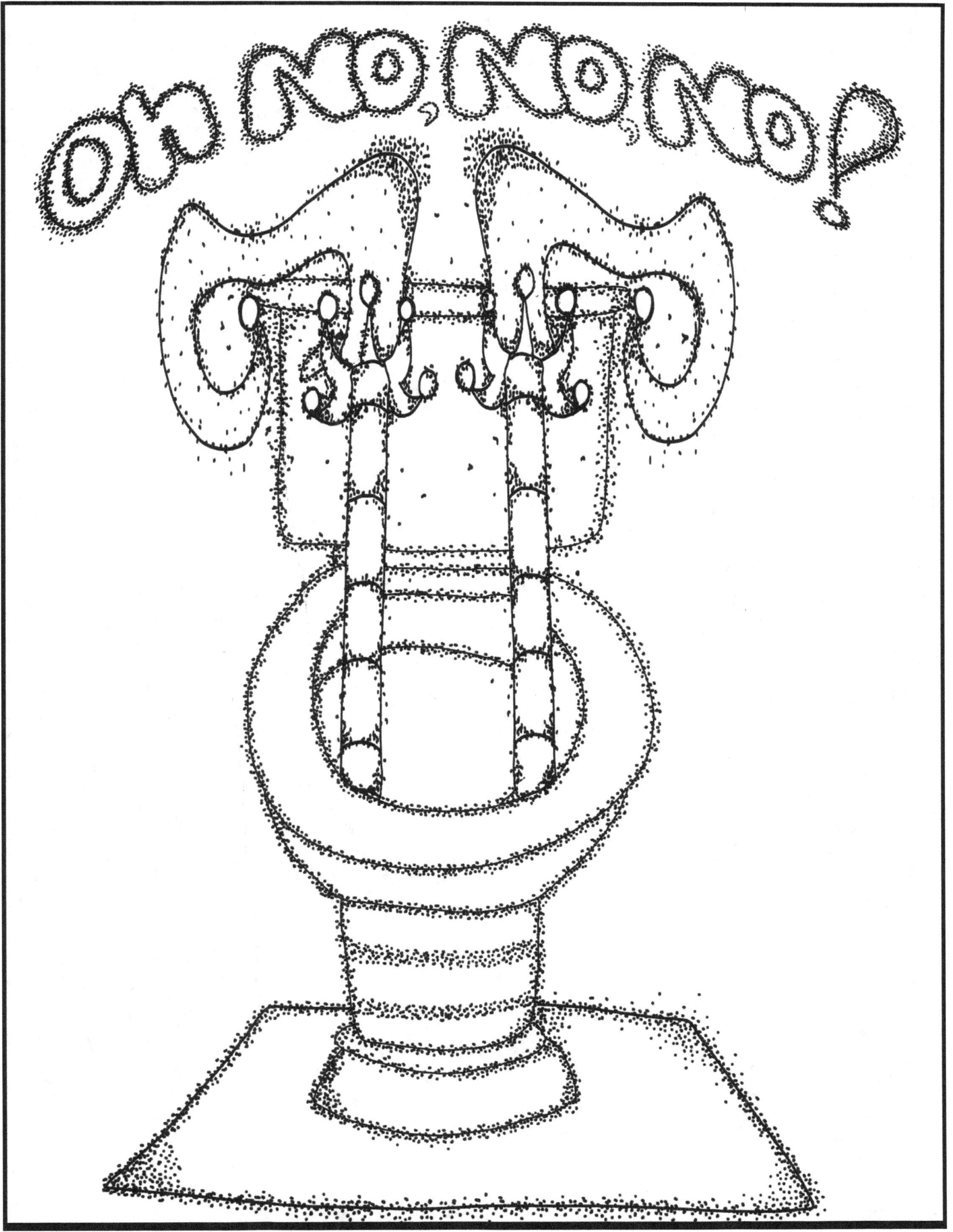
Oh No, No, No?

Oh
no,
no,
no!
GET
OUT
of
THERE

Rest
in peace?
Not
with this
Elf
around
you never can
tell
where next he'll
be found!

Oh this
Elf
who should
have
stayed on
the shelf
did not
realize
he would
end this
story
himself!

Elf's
Last
Move
R I P

This Elf
is just silly
and likes
to have
fun!
He is
really
wishing
good things
for
EVERYONE
!!!!!!!

Merry
Christmas

Merry
Christmas
D. McDonald Designs
That Elf Ain't On the Shelf
Christmas Coloring Book

Elf in A Cone
D. McDonald Designs
That Elf Ain't On the Shelf
Christmas Coloring Book
Amazon
Deborah L. McDonald

D. McDonald Designs
HOLIDAY COLORING BOOK FOR
GOING TO BE A DOGGONE GREAT HOLIDAY!
WOOF
Merry Christmas!
Peace On Earth
Be Cool

D. McDonald Designs
Have A Handmade Holiday
2018
Christmas Coloring
Book Six Angels

Merry Christmas

Have
A
Curly
Swirly
Christmas
Coloring
Book

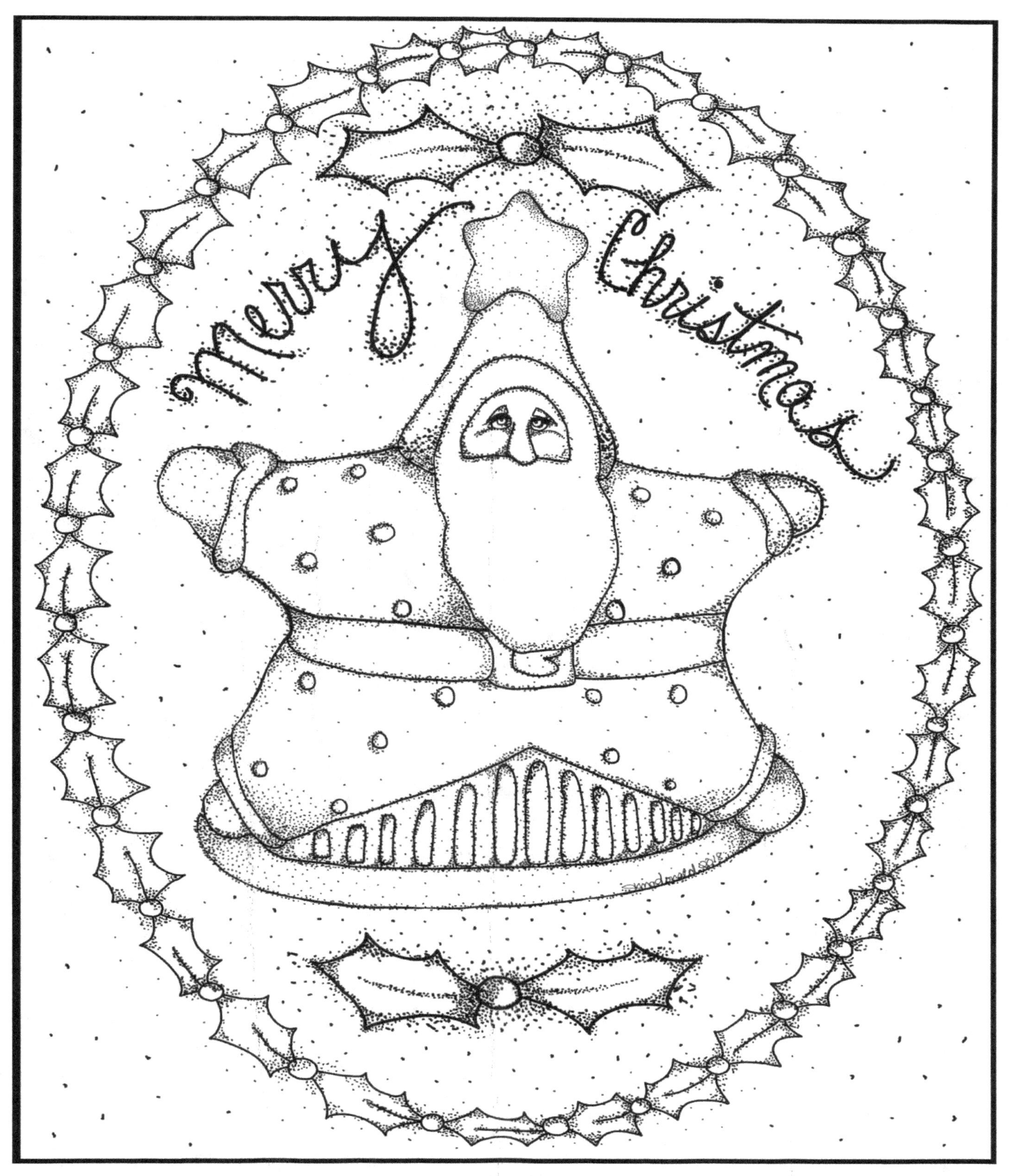

Merry Christmas
D. McDonald Designs
Have A Handmade Holiday
Christmas Coloring Book One

D. McDonald Designs
Have A Handmade Holiday
Christmas Coloring Book One

D. McDonald Designs
Have A Handmade Holiday
Christmas Coloring
Book Three

Merry Christmas

D. McDonald Designs
Have A Handmade Holiday
Christmas Coloring Book Four

D. McDonald Designs
That Elf Ain't On the Shelf
Christmas Coloring Book Two

D.McDonald Designs
Christmas Coloring Book 2017

That Elf Ain't on the Shelf
Christmas Coloring Book Two
I was sunnyside up until........
That elf took a jump
off the shelf!

That Elf Ain't on the Shelf Christmas Coloring Book Two

Crazy Christmas Trees & More Adult Coloring Book

Bundle Up Because Baby It's Cold Out Side

Deborah L. McDonald Amazon

Christmas Coloring Book 2017

That Elf Ain't on the Shelf Coloring Story Book
Amazon by: Deborah L. McDonald

Books
by
Deborah L. McDonald
Fabulous Florals Adult Coloring Book
Fabulous Florals Two Adult Coloring Book
D. McDonald Designs
Gems & Gypsies Coloring Work Book
Celebrating A Very Colorful Birthday!
It's My Birthday Party Coloring Book
D. McDonald Designs
Magical Mandala Coloring Book
D. McDonald Designs
Mandala Coloring Book
D. McDonald Designs
Peace & Love
Adult & Children's Coloring Book
D. McDonald Designs
Happy Halloween
Adult & Children's Coloring Book
PICTURE PUZZLES ACTIVITY COLORING BOOK
Find the difference
Over 40 designs to search for differences or color the same from left to right to increase focusing skills!
D. McDonald Designs
PICTURE PUZZLES ACTIVITY COLORING BOOK TWO
A wonderful memory work out for all ages
Branching Out
D. McDonald Designs
dmcdonald's Full Page Size
Mysteria
A place where Everything is another
dmcdonald designs publication
Welcome to My Garden Coloring Book
D. Mc Donald Designs
Toddler Time Color & Learn Series
Book One
Featuring No Fail Friendly Black
D. McDonald Designs
Butterflies, Bugs, and Black Background
A Family
D. McDonald Designs
Deb Dragons One Coloring Book
Cards for all occasions and coloring pages all ages
Cake For Breakfast
Deluxe Edition
d.mcdonald designs
Cakes, Castles, Outer Space
White & Black Backgrounds Edition
Adult & Children's Coloring Book
Gears, Gizmos, Outer Space and More Adult & Children's Coloring Book

Elf Sunnyside Up Eggs

FIND
DEBORAH L. MCDONALD
ON
FACEBOOK
D.MCDONALD DESIGNS
COLORING CLUB
TO SEE PAGE
BY PAGE FLIP THRU
TOURS..... JUST ASK,
SOME GOOD PERSON
WILL DIRECT YOU
TO WHERE!

Please
Be
Kind
and
Return
to
Amazon
and
give this
book
some
stars
and a review
and perhaps
share a few pages
you colored!
Thanks!
J.McDonald

Wonderful, Whimsical, Wacky Wreaths
Adult Coloring Book
Deborah L. McDonald
Amazon